*Compassionate Travel*

for M T Kelly

*Compassionate Travel*

*J D Carpenter*

Black Moss Press

©J.D. Carpenter, 1994

Published by Black Moss Press
2450 Byng Road
Windsor, Ontario
N8W 3E8

Black Moss books are distributed
in Canada and the United States by
Firefly Books Ltd.
250 Sparks Avenue, Willowdale, Ontario, M2H 2S4
All orders should be directed there.

Financial assistance toward the publication of this book has been gratefully received from the Canada Council, the Department of Communications and the Ontario Arts Council.

Canadian Cataloguing in Publication data:

Carpenter, J. D.
  Compassionate Travel

Poems.
ISBN 0-88753-243-8

I. Title

PS8555.A7616C65   1994   C811'.54   C94-900390-5
PR9199.3.C37C65   1994

The cover photo was taken by the author in Toledo, Spain.

Some of the poems in this collection have appeared in the following publications: *Acanthus, Ariel, Canadian Literature, County Magazine, The Fiddlehead, Northward Journal.*

## Contents

| | |
|---|---|
| 8 | Compassionate Travel |
| 10 | Paddy |
| 14 | Ranch in Winter |
| 15 | Gull Pond |
| 16 | Corn Road |
| 18 | The Vineyard |
| 19 | Nocturne |
| 20 | Surfer Girl |
| 21 | Soloist |
| 22 | Book of Love |
| | |
| 26 | The Black Ponds |
| 27 | Long Lake |
| 28 | Lake Superior |
| 31 | Tobermory |
| 32 | Marathons in Jeopardy |
| 34 | Middle Leg, Missinaibi |
| 36 | Our Northern Tour |
| | |
| 44 | Our Southern Tour |
| 48 | Massachusetts |
| 51 | Condo |
| 52 | Carreglwyd |
| 54 | North Wales |
| 55 | Rue Bosquet |
| 56 | Chartres |
| 57 | Postcard |
| 58 | Two Seas |

Other books of poetry by J D Carpenter:

*Nightfall, Ferryland Head,* Missing Link Press, 1976
*Swimming At Twelve Mile,* Penumbra Press, 1979
*Lakeview*, Black Moss Press, 1990

I

## COMPASSIONATE TRAVEL

I shower in the dark.
Like a blind man, I know

where everything is
— soap, towel, cloth.


I had a blind friend once
who lived above a pharmacy.

His lights were always off,
even at night when I came

to collect his empties.
He lived like a mole.


I drive you to the airport.
We speed along the highway,

white headlights and red
tail-lights and yellow

foglights, like Chinese
checkers against the night.


You are in blue air now,
above the three-days cloud-cover

that keeps the rest of us
hopping and spitting

like water simmering
under a lid.

A thousand miles away
your father is dying.

Is he in darkness
already? Is he in pain,

is he frightened?
And you. Are you calm?

What are your eyes
looking at — a magazine,

a cup of coffee, the view
from your window

Or are they shut,
like mine?

# PADDY

I

In Midgic, New Brunswick — a town so small
the only noises you hear this bleak November

morning are the crunch of gravel beneath
your feet, wheel-squeak of a baby carriage,

distant barking — the only high-rise
(four storeys) is a rooming-house

for alcoholics. The woman who lived next door
to your father claims she knew him well,

but we see too much of him in her
 — the cigarettes, the resignation —

and decline her *kaffeeklatsch*. Other residents,
shadowy behind curtains, watch us carry

boxes and bags to the car. In the kitchen
I pour the last of his Wiser's down the drain;

he would have had me drink it. Room to room
you wander through his things, numbed

by what you see: your photo on the TV,
his respirator, drawers full of cufflinks

and dirty jokes, the unmade bed, a pair
of soiled green trousers on the bathroom tiles.

We empty cupboards and closets. We empty
the refrigerator of the left-overs of the last

meal he cooked for himself. When we have done
all we can, still you will not leave.

## II

People Paddy knew offer us a room
in their farmhouse. The man drives

the school bus; the woman works
in the post office. Their children

are grown and gone. We make a circuit
— Port Elgin, Sackville, Midgic,

Moncton — looking after things:
insurance, will, rent, car.

The ladieswear shop in Sackville
doubles as a telephone depositary.

"Return it to Reen's Fashions
on Bridge Street," the operator says.


## III

Legion members brush off berets, dust
blue blazers, stand to attention

as *The Last Post* is played. Your Irish
father was a chauffeur in Belgium

when he met your mother. He drove
the British brass around. Your Irish

father took me to my first bar
— the Todmorden on Pottery Road;

we drank draft all afternoon with a detective
he knew. He got me a job and found me a car.

When I asked his permission to marry you,
his bearhug was one part love, one part warning.

People we will never see again press our hands.
They take us to a Petit Cap diner for clams.

The minister is there — fiftyish,
wall-eyed, the type of bachelor

you wouldn't trust your children to;
voluble, articulate, deaf in one ear.

"I've been transferred to the coast."
Others — I don't remember who.


IV

The funeral director in Sackville
was a farmer till a blizzard killed

his cattle. He grieved so hard
he made it his business. While we wait

at the crematorium (he has the urn),
sorrow shuts us down.


V

We drive beside the Saint John River.
Your father's ashes are on the back seat

of his burgundy Cutlass Supreme
in a carton that once held T-shirts from Korea.

We stay at a motel in Fredericton.
From the pool come the screams

of a female high school volleyball team.
In the morning, surrounded by six-footers,

we eat pancakes in the motel restaurant.
They energize us, these girls,

and we push on into Quebec.  Smoked meat
in Montreal.  Sleet in Dorion.  That night,

in the washroom of a truck-stop near Cornwall,
a Georgia cowboy punches the comb dispenser.

Outside, rigs pant like sled dogs
in their traces.  We are taking Paddy home.

# RANCH IN WINTER

Across the road ten deer forage
in the horse field, flags erect.

The horses — Scout, Blue, Blaze,
Lady, Reno, Joy — are absent,

wintering at Glenora, fat and furry;
forgotten are the tourists waiting

their turns in the dust of Jack's
corral, his enormous radio

hauling soft rock
across the lake from Rochester.


Below the house my dog finds
a snow-bridge over the little creek

that appears and disappears like a broken line.
The bay is still a desert of ice,

and we climb the ice dunes along the shore.
Soon, the thunderous break-up will begin,

scaups and old-squaws will doze and preen
on the open water, and tourists

will stand in the dust of Jack's coral,
choosing their horses, asking their names.

# GULL POND

The lane to Gull Pond is stony,
and Oblio, shoeless, prefers

the softer going along the ditch,
but the tall grass conceals holes

that make him stumble, and bottles
and boards that break beneath his hooves.

I pull him out and we turn back,
the neighbours' barking dog darting

in front of us like a jet-ski.
Another day, I suppose. Gull Pond

by car, like those youngsters who
drive there to drink and fumble

in the sawgrass, the moonlight,
music thumping from their radios

while sea-birds whirl in the darkness,
white and invisible, a thousand miles from the sea.

# CORN ROAD

Driving through the corn to our trailer
is like passing between ranks of soldiers

who tower above us, ears hanging
from their belts like grenades, banging

dangerously against our mirrors.
Standing on the picnic table

we listen to the stalks rub and whisper
like dresses. The breeze makes the corn talk.

To the children of the farmer who works our land
(whose corn this is), there is no need

for comparisons — corn to silk or soldiers:
things are what they appear to be.


The children sell vegetables at roadside:
tomatoes, peppers, beans. They sit

two to a chair, and push and argue and laugh.
They perch in the bed of their father's half-ton

(except the youngest, asleep in the crook
 of his arm) as he hauls feed to his heifers.

Everything interests them: people who stop;
the crash that killed their cousin.

Things are what they appear to be:
tomatoes, heifers, absence. There are no

levels of meaning, only the article itself:
a road through corn; Josh asleep

in the crook of his father's arm;
a dead boy's handsome colour cameo.

# THE VINEYARD

The old gelding stands like a statue
in the wheatfield, black on yellow.

He is such a pet he wanders at will,
and tourists are always reporting

a loose horse.  It is evening,
and the sky turns cartwheels of colour

— purple and salmon and green.
I lean on my hoe in the vineyard.

Overhead, herons follow their flight path
home from the lake.  Near me,

a kingbird perches on a bamboo stake.
I resolve to do one more row.


In the morning a passing truck
startles a doe out of the bush.

From the vineyard I watch her
teeter-totter through the wheat,

then slow to a walk, and all I can see
are her ears pushing forward like periscopes.

I turn back to my tending.
When I asked my farmer what he thought of us

making wine in the County, he said,
"No one else 'round here grows grapes."

But we'll persist.  We want to drink
for free when we're old.

# NOCTURNE

Harvest time, and the combines
work at night.  We mistake

the flash of headlights
as they turn at the end of a row

for lightning, or the beacon
of the Salmon Point lighthouse.


When we are ready for bed,
we kill the lamp in its litter

of moths on the table,
go inside the trailer,

and ride to sleep
on the distant drone of engines.

## SURFER GIRL

The only weddings you go to these days
are second marriages. The speeches
have improved, the settings are more opulent,

and the music decade-specific.
On the dance floor the grey-haired men
crooning "Surfer Girl" into the ears

of their wives later agree (drunkenly,
 on the terrace) to unhang their skates
and play Tuesday night non-contact over-forty shinny.


On the subway home, you are a small band of civility
crossing the desert of your city. You hope
the kids have left some pizza. The dog

will need a walk. The lyrics to "Feelings"
coat your brain; you grow morose. You think
about the dead, the dying, the past.

"Feelings, nothing more than feelings,"
you sob, as your wife guides you along
the platform and up the stairs, to the street.

## SOLOIST

In 'Glory Train' she moves her fists
backwards and forwards like the side

rods on an old locomotive. This is all
the dancing she does, but when she was

fourteen, before she found religion,
she must have been a picture, hand

jiving in front of her mirror,
Aretha on the phonograph:

"Sock it to me, sock it to me,
 sock it to me, sock it to me."


And when she plays the blues
on her Fender Jazzmaster in 'Oh Mary,

Don't You Weep' — behind her the swaying
chorus, dressed, like her, in brown

and burgundy gowns — her voice
is the perfect extension, and there she is

in her bedroom again, B B King on the radio,
and she's listening, she's learning:

"Sweet little angel,
I love the way you spread your wings."


                    — Montreal Jubilation Gospel Choir,
                       Picton United Church, July, 1992

# BOOK OF LOVE

I

Our children are so homegrown they think
your Europeanness quaint.  But how exotic

you were in 1967, with your starched blouses
your *Noily Prat*, the dark and polished house

you took me to: your parents, your poodles,
your Friday feasts of head cheese, Belgian

beer and French fries with mayonnaise.
Like a throng of tiny witnesses, knickknacks

crowded the platerail, the mantlepiece;
they certainly saw more than your snoring father

did, but your mother, watchful in the smoky
blue glow of the television set, saw all.

II

Last night I was the one with enough energy
to wait up for our son driving home from

a concert outside the city.  The roads
were icy, and after I'd flipped through

as many channels as were necessary
to know there was nothing on

— like solitaire — and after I'd read
as much of a magazine as my eyes could bear,

there was nothing for it but to stand
in the darkened livingroom, watch taxis

slide through the stop at our corner,
and wait for the sweep of his headlights.


III


He was two when we bought this house
(or, rather, when you bought it, since I

was gallivanting around Ireland at the time),
and now a woman from the insurance company

wants our shingles replaced.  Just because
our windows are grimy and we use piggy banks

and 8-tracks to prop them open, just because
our Christmas lights are up all year

and the cellar smells of rabbit shit
and retriever, no one can call us negligent.

Our children are our show.  Where once
we were two, now we are four.  We overflow.


IV


Saturday mornings, driving to "riding",
our daughter allows me my jazz show.

We discuss which horses we would buy
if we had a place to keep them.

While she tacks up, I let the dog loose
through the fields.  All week long

he's imprisoned in the yard; this is his
chance to run wild.  On our way home,

our daughter dials an oldies station.
We play "Name That Tune" and sing along:

"Oh, I wonder, wonder who, be-do-oo-oo
— who wrote the Book of Love?"


V


I am Christmas shopping today.  The perfume
I buy costs twice what our rings did

twenty years ago.  On a whim I board
the Queen Street trolley and ride it past

the asylum, the courthouse, the vendors
and beggars on the sidewalks, and the beach

at Sunnyside where, as a child, I attended
picnics and birthdays.  At the end of the line,

the driver says, "You can transfer
onto Long Branch, and that'll take you

to the city limits, or pay another fare,
and I'll take you back where you came from."

II

## THE BLACK PONDS

In the lean-to five men lie abreast,
a smouldering fire at their feet.

For warmth they bury their heads
in their sleeping-bags. They look

like disaster dead, laid out
on the floor of a gym. The wolf's

sharp bark, the grouse's drum
(which they feel but cannot hear),

Miss October pinned to the crossbar
— all these inform their dreams.


When they wake, their bedding
is white with frost. They see

the moon as a lemon wedge
and the stars as effervescence

in the tall black drink of the night.
Shotguns up their backs,

they wade through dripping darkness
— past moose scat, antler rub —

to the ponds near the iron mine,
and wait for the colour to come.

## LONG LAKE

Beside the fire Bert fiddles
with his new hearing-aids.

Bear dogs with radio sensor collars
come sniffing through our camp.

We shoo them. We are cool
to their high-tech masters.

A man in an orange cap walks
through, a pheasant hanging

upside down from his fingers,
its feathers up around its ears

like the petticoats
of a woman hanged by her heels.

Bert takes a picture
of our group in front

of the lean-to, and another
of a dead wood duck propped

against a rock. When its head
flops back drunkenly, everyone

laughs at the cigarette
pointing skyward like a shotgun.

I row out on the lake.
The water is deep and black.

If a man wanted to die,
he could do worse than Long Lake

on a sunny fall day, bright leaves
dropping like petals on his chest.

# LAKE SUPERIOR

(for Peter Curtis)

I


We camp in a stand of red pine
at Gargantua. Our neighbours

are mergansers and loons.
A stone's throw from our beach,

the cylinder head of the *Columbus*
rises above the water like a

deadhead. From the lookout
we can see the islands offshore

— Wide, Peerless, Dixon,
and far to the south, Leach,

flat as a plate, whose trees
are spines on Misshepezhieu's back.


II


We paddle the blue-green chop
to the distant ochre cliff

of Devil's Warehouse. "It may be
we will touch the Happy Isles,"

my sternsman sings, "And see
the great Achilles, whom we knew."

Behind us, a cloud-shadow slips
like a veil down the perfect brow

of the cape. On a bare volcanic shoal,
harebells bloom in the mustard-coloured lichen,

and bumblebees, miles from home,
hum like air-conditioners.

An hour north — rolling channels,
beaches of black sand, an inland lake,

and Devil's Chair, through whose window
we watch a golden, guano-covered rock

that makes my friend recall the slopes
of Sicily, their flows of white houses.


III


On a wall inside a cabin on the bay,
these words are written: "This building

was the office for the fishing business
of Jack Lawrence McKay. Built in 1948

and occupied until 1961. After that
he sold this area of 65,000 acres

and moved to California. The waterfront
was occupied by six cottages, docks, twine

house, cookery. His family returned
on July 26, 1992, in memorial."

Also written: "The crew of the *Norah*,
Laingsburg, Michigan, 8-29-86";

"Verdun Venn / 1955 / 1990
(revisit 35 years later)"; "The crew

of the *Dispatch II,* Sept 8/86"; and,
"Giving up smoking to-day May 21/80.

Archie." And this reply:
"You are full of shit Archie."


IV


Then south, past Rhyolite Cove,
Telegraph Rock, Bald Head,

Katherine Cove, Sand River
and the Lizard Islands,

past black spruce and yellow birch,
butterwort and tamarack

to much older graffiti
on a granite shelf at Agawa:

"Twin bears"; "Myeengun's war party
with crane, eagle and turtle";

"Horse and rider and four spheres";
"Misshepezhieu, canoe and serpents".

# TOBERMORY

In the clear cold water of Big Tub Harbour
my hand, toplit like an aquarium exhibit,

white as a dead man's, touches
the wooden windlass of the *Sweepstakes*.

Above me, glass-bottomed tour boats circle;
below-decks, zealous in their get-ups,

teams of divers clamber
like white-handed gibbons; bouquets

of bubbles bloom
through the schooner's planking.

Ninety feet away
the *City of Grand Rapids* lies.

Less popular — no hatches to swim through,
her hold silt-ridden — her only visitors

are a solitary bass, hanging motionless
above the boiler, and a shoal

of silver minnows that glitter
in the sun like spoons.

Early next morning I swim to the tug
*Bob Foote* to read her draught-markings,

to see her "bow-stem rise gracefully
above the north end of the wreck",

but other divers appear, tour boats
gather, and a car ferry bellows

and begins her day, sliding by me
like the skyline of a city.

# MARATHONS IN JEOPARDY

At dawn loons called, and Finn went down
to the water to wash, and slipped and popped

his knee. All morning he paddled in agony,
and when he couldn't go on, we found

some fish 'n' fly boys from Jersey
("You nice people up here," they said),

who radioed for help. All afternoon
Finn lay in his tent with Pushkin, biscuits

and whiskey, islanded by pain. At dusk
we heard a drone, and watched the seaplane

duck under storm clouds
to pluck our patient from us.

We ate in silence, pike bones
catching like tripwires in our voices.


In the morning we left the lake
and began the river descent. We camped at

Thread the Needle, Ruthie's Run and Little Pinetree.
During a rain we made a classroom of the forest:

goldthread, bed straw, sensitive fern;
ostrich, oak and royal fern; interrupted fern

and sweet gale; spinulose and horsetail;
and juncos begging cheese at our breadboard paddle.

The last set of rapids was a two-mile boil
foaming into a postcard lake. At lunch

we upended a paddle in the sand
and drank a toast to melon-kneed Finn

(long since entrained for the city
 — spouting Shakespeare in a redcap's ear).

Then the last short haul to the highway.
Piping us from Wenebegon, a flypast of osprey.

# MIDDLE LEG, MISSINAIBI

I

Spirits rousing themselves
are mist on the water.

An early hot sun dapples
the river bank.  We break camp,

run two small rapids,
listen to a marsh hawk chitter,

a red squirrel scold us,
dead cedar creak in the forest.

A wading moose carries his rack
like a tray of drinks.

*Old Sam Peabody Peabody Peabody!*
a white-throat sings.

Mergansers fly in formation,
inches above the water.

A golden-eye herds her chicks
and dives, and they all dive.


II

Pond Falls, Devil Cap,
Devil Shoepack, and the long

rock garden of Albany Rapids.
Near Glassy Falls Pepsi cans

begin to appear
beneath my paddle's flash.

Five miles from Mattice,
drifting the last short stretch

to the highway, we stop
at a Cree cemetery.

The graves are in ruins.
The pickets of the fences

lean crazily on each other.
But someone has come

to make repairs — a box
of nails, the hammer on the stump.

Whoever it was
has seen us coming,

dropped his tools,
and vanished into the trees.

# OUR NORTHERN TOUR

Put in
— Mattice

Osprey
— mile 2

Hipdeep in wildflowers
— Rock Island portage

Our guide reads *Flaming Carrot Comics*
— mile 5

Pink rose petals
— Black Feather Rapids

The river wraps us
around the rock
— Kettle Falls

Dreams of my children
— Alice Island

Mystery shape ashore
turns out to be
perfect conical sandcastle
(tiny flag at its peak)
— mile 29

Sculpture: balanced
on the roof of a boulder as big
as a bungalow, a tangle of spring flood timber
— mile 42

Inside the derelict cabin:
a bottle of Mountain White Chablis,
empty; a full bottle of French dressing
four years past its 'best before';

a chipmunk
— mile 49

Queen Anne's lace six feet high
— micro-climate, Thunderhouse portage

Where
if you don't watch out
you die
— Thunderhouse Falls

Cliff diving
— Conjuring House Rock

Joe Collins and Ed Lewis
of St Joseph, Michigan, miss
the portage, capsize
— Stone Rapids

Under the foodpack, I slip
in moosemud, come up
like a black man
— Long Rapids portage

Drinking Jack
with Joe Collins:
"I went to school
with Jack Daniel's granddaughter."
— Long Rapids camp

Where
in 1974
John Bemrose
found the body
of a boy from Kansas City:
barefoot, blue sweatshirt,
stench, bloat
— Bull Moose Bay

Mulligatawny
— mile 72

Where
in 1776
Thomas Atkinson
and a small party
of Englishmen and Indians
held siege against winter
after struggling upriver
(56 days, 120 miles)
from Moosefort
in the search
for furs
   — Wapiscogamy House

Wooden cross
picket fence
mark grave of
BABY JOSEPH MARTEN
May 6–September 4
         1925
   — Pivabiska Creek

Dream the taxi
home from the station
gets lost in city streets
   — 5th camp

Wings
singing, an
immature sandhill crane
   — mile 89

Pizza:
cubed salami
chopped onion
tomato sauce
gorilla cheese
on bannock
   — mile 100

Chittering
tree to tree,

kingfishers escort us
  — Giant Spruce Island

Paddle (naked) to the sea
  — Opasatika River

Behind the palisades
of spruce and poplar
along each side of the river,
endless bog and the nightmare noises
  — dusk, Water Cabin

Our guide says, "Mmmm,
  love that 'may contain' meat."
  — morning, Water Cabin

Yahooing through
  — McCuaig Creek Rapids

Headwinds force a halt:
we huddle like cattle,
backs to the rain
  — mile 121

Trembling in the tent,
its walls alive with lightning,
we sip the last of the bourbon
  — 8th camp

Confluence of rivers:
Missinaibi+Mattagami=Moose
  — Portage Island

From the trestle
Cree children rain
pebbles on our picnic:
"Get off our land!"
  — Moose River Crossing

Grey geese
  — Grey goose Island

Gypsum caves
— mile 153

Gyrfalcon
— Mike Island

The northern lights
lifting like a curtain
— mile 163

So cold
I sleep with my ballcap on
— Little Asp Island

Red-breasted merganser
and young
— Baby Island

Twelve maps down, one to go
— mile 170

After the roller-coaster ride
my cup on the bow
is full of water
— Kwataboahegan Rapids

River as wide as the world
— mile 177

Air show: arctic terns
— 10th camp

Rain
for the tenth day
of eleven
— Bushy Island

Lunch: corned beef balls
peanut butter balls
— mile 183

Our guide sings, "I've come
to take you home, whoo hoo."
(Talking Heads, 'Swamp')
— mile 190

Three canoes abreast, we sail
(shower curtain, tent fly,
 mylar blanket) the last leg
— Moosonee

The tripper
from *Pays d'en Haut*
tells us five died last year,
four (mapless, thinking it was just
 another rapids) at Thunderhouse Falls
 — freighter canoe taxi, Charles Island

Cold beer
— Polar Bear Lodge

1.      In
      Loving
      Memory
       of
     Jane Caroline
      Guaghigan
    Born April 10 1913
    Died April 20 1921
"There is a home for little children
  Above the bright blue skies"

2.       M
       A
       R.
       10
      WILLIE
       M
       O
       O
       R
       E

3. Roy John Suthrlnd

4.  Alfred Louttit          16 Yrs.
    Tommy      "            15 "
    Jimmy Sutherland        15 "
    Arthur     "            15 "
    John Sailor's           11 Yrs
    Roderick Wascowin       9 Yrs
    Sinclair Napanee        9 "

      Pupils of Moosefort
       Boarding School
     Accidental Drowning
       July 19, 1919
       Asleep in Jesus
— epitaphs, St Thomas Anglican Church, Moose Factory

Tide
— James Bay

Last portage: wharf to train
— Moosonee

Tourists
— Polar Bear Express

Egg rolls
beef fried rice
beef with tomato
shrimp with garlic
chicken soo guy
cream pie
coffee
  — Gold Star Restaurant, Cochrane

Entrain
— Porquis Junction

III

## OUR SOUTHERN TOUR

*He carried his camera all the time even until the last.*
— Lee Friedlander on E. J. Bellocq, photographer of Storyville prostitutes, circa 1912.

*Child's grave, Hale County, Alabama, 1936.*
*Negro houses, outskirts of Tupelo, Mississippi, 1936.*
*Breakfast room, Belle Grove Plantation, White Chapel,*
　　　　*Louisiana, 1935.*
— captions for photographs, Walker Evans.


I


Purple gorse
　— Hadley, Pennsylvania

Amish farmer, dirt road
　— Zelienople

Peanuts and beer, on bar
　— Mars

Ferryman
　— Ohio River at Sly

Old man on store porch, rocking
　— Frenchburg, Kentucky

Negroes in bed of pick-up truck, graveyard
　— Lexington

Sham, Tell, List,
Jaipur, Bagdad, Damascus,
Assagai, Ack Ack, Never Bend,
Gallant Man, Hoist the Flag
　— stallions, Clairborne and Spendthrift Farms

Downpour, highway
— Horse Cave

Antique dealer posing in her living-room
— Nashville, Tennessee

Mansion, splendid in ruin
— Macon, Mississippi

Fishing for channel cat
— Lake Pontchartrain

Perspiring man
— Metairie

Magnolias
— Carondelet Avenue, New Orleans

Iron Lace
— Dauphin Street, Vieux Carré

Cajun minstrels
— Decatur Street

Tourists and lawnchairs in line
for sternwheeler *Natchez*
— Toulouse Street Wharf

O'Neill Watts, Jr., Washington Thomas, Lionel Brown
— cabbies' names on cab doors, Royal Street

Red beans and rice
— diner, Burgundy Street

Stucco, terracotta, armoured palms
— Prytania Avenue, the Garden District

Shards of glass in courtyard walls
— Cadiz Avenue

Wall panels (Louis XIV) of red damask, brocaded;
frescoed ceilings, signed *de Rudder, Paris, 1958*
— the Williams mansion, St Charles Avenue

Pool Players
— Blackie's Lounge, Lockport

*Ramona Mae, Thunder Shower, June Reed,
Misfit, Outer Limits*
— Cocodrie Bayou

Barefoot man shoveling shrimp
— Cocodrie

Arc Welder
— Houma

Alligator in ditch
— Pecan Island

Gulls hovering for food
— Port Bolivar ferry, Texas

Obese man at desk
— lobby, S.S. Snort Motel, Galveston

Frame house, horses on beach
— Galveston


II


Sinking cabin
— Atchafalaya Swamp, Louisiana

Jimmy Stewart in "Shenandoah"
— motel TV, Baton Rouge

Crab parts
— beach at Biloxi, Mississippi

Man urinating into swimming-pool, evening
— campground, Hope Hull, Alabama

Bearded trees, brook, bridge
— near Fayetteville, Georgia

Policemen frisking Negro
— streetcorner, Atlanta

Woman in sneakers, apron
— Caney Branch, Tennessee

Loose horse, highway
— Bluefield, Virginia

The burning sky
— Beckley, West Virginia

The putting to sleep of the land
— Hadley, Pennsylvania

# MASSACHUSETTS

I

Cormorants crowd the wires at Nauset.
At Race Point swimmers float on the sea's

cold boil.  A bartender in Hyannis
explains his failure at the seminary:

"There was one vow I couldn't take,
you can guess what it is."  He asks if we

know how eskimos pee, and thumbs an ice cube
across the room.  On Commercial Street

in Provincetown, gay men walk hand in hand
past boutiques and cafes, past old salts

dozing in the porch-shade
of their cedar shake Cape Cod homes.


II

At Fenway, Tom Brunansky almost lands
in our laps chasing Winfield's wrong-field

liner to right.  At the aquarium on the pier,
Lowell's "cowed, compliant fish" drift past

our faces.  In Boston Common, my mother's
friend's photograph, taken a year ago

through a tour bus window, cannot compare
to the article itself: St. Gaudens' bronze

relief of "Colonel Shaw and his bell-cheeked
Negro infantry". At Rosy O'Grady's Blind Pig

Saloon, the bartender has a rubber ear, and
the doorknob lies forgotten on the floor.



III


A monument in Barre lists the names
of the town's Civil War dead: Baxter King

was killed at Lynchburg, Emerson Mullett
at Spotsylvania, Porter Robinson at New

Market; others at Gettysburg, Petersburg,
Fredericksburg, Antietam, Cold Harbor.

Half died of disease: fever, rheumatism.
Sunstroke took George Moran at Harpers Ferry.

Nelson Young died a prisoner
of war in Andersonville, Georgia.

"Disease" killed Privates Tooley, Varney
and Goddard, still training in Barre.



IV


Some towns in central Massachusetts:
Old Furnace, New Braintree, Belchertown,

Griswoldville, Nipmuck Pond, Phillipston
Four Corners. At a Mobil station outside

Greenfield, Billie Sneed, extradition agent,
feeds two cuffed prisoners in her van:

"We're taking the one fellow, the forger,
to Geneva, Illinois," she says, "and the boy

in the red shirt to Orlando, Florida."
Coastal names include Squantum, Pocasset,

Cohasset, Salem, Sea View, Wellfleet,
Falmouth, Yarmouth, Newbury Old Town.


V


From a window of the Howard Johnson in Cambridge
I watch scullers on the Charles River,

not far from where Faulkner's Quentin
drowned himself: "then you will remember

that for you to go to harvard has been
your mothers dream since you were born

and no compson has ever disappointed a lady".
A bartender on River Street whispers into the ear

of the man asleep on a stool: "Pilot
to bombardier, pilot to bombardier."

On a trapeze above Harvard Square, a man
juggles torches. A crowd watches.

## CONDO

Our hummingbird, a Cuban Emerald,
is so sure of herself my Minolta

in *macro* does not budge her
from the oleander.  She is not ours,

of course, any more than is
the third green of the golf course,

which is our balcony view; or the yachts
in the basin; or the hearty welcome

of the *Pisces* maitre d'; or the mockingbird
atop the thatch palm beside the pool,

running through his repertoire; or
the octopus and angelfish at Bootle Bay.


Nor are the children at West End ours,
sullen and taunting in red and white

uniforms as they kick their dusty way;
nor the mountains of gutted conch, pink

and obscene in the sun; nor the littered
graves at Eight Mile Rock; nor the rudeness

of cashiers; nor the brazenness of young men
selling drugs *inside* the Pantry Pride; nor

the failed resorts; nor the drunks, nor
the cripples, nor the ditches choked

with garbage on the roads that lead
nowhere.  None of this is ours.

— Freeport, Bahamas

# CARREGLWYD

In this heart of fields
a small wood stands: cloud of green

in a yellow sky. And in the wood
the great stone house

— its apron of lawn
boat-house and lily-padded pond.

Sheep people the fields
like little cars. Nettles prick.

Horse breach the fences
to reach the farmer's barley.

On a far rise, a ruin.
Broken bells in bush, two gazebos lean.

At the footbridge, a row of weasels
and stoats, spiked on barbs, shrivel

and dry; hedgehogs hunch in death
like sea-plants; spiders cloak the head

and eyes of a jackdaw jammed
on branches. It is a medieval place.

In the house, the dead glower
from the walls, wasps beat their heads

against the window-panes,
and Cook rants in the kitchen.

In the punt on the pond, we row to the weir
and back to the bank. The springer barks.

The children bowl on the grass,
Willow snorts from a dank and cluttered stall,

and Lulu nods in her wheelchair — waiting,
like this house, for a final end to things.

# NORTH WALES

In the sheep and hawk hills of Llangollen
we make our camp.  Shards of shale

lie about us like the stony pies
of some mad baker.  Sheep roam

where houses were, where halls
and bedrooms stood, and lambs lie

where lovers lay — in the loins of hills.
Above us stars congregate,

and in the distance the lights of valley towns waver.
Whiskey gone, we slide to sleep,

not so much men in an eyrie of hawks
as eyes in a head, babes at the breast.

# RUE BOSQUET

Here we sit, smug in Paris, above the boulevard.
About the room in metal boxes — small cigars.

From the balcony, umbrellas and small cars
move like coloured fish

through trees that sway like fans of coral
in corridors of the sea.

This landscape, these trees
yield like lovers

to the perfect insertion and arc of love.
Wreckage of supper lies across our plates,

and wine, standing, dies in glasses.  And
here we sit, smug in Paris, above the boulevard.

# CHARTRES

We walk back down from the fabulous glass,
past the costumed women selling lace,

through a steep narrow street of stone shops,
across the square, past the station, to the park.

The rain resumes, and we clatter a broad pavilion,
open our lunch of eggs and cheese, apples and bread,

spread it among the dead leaves.  We watch
the sun return, an old man walk his dog,

and pilgrimage women — down from the spires
and statuary, down near an implement shed —

lean their canes and crutches among hoes and rakes,
hike their skirts, squat and water the earth.

## POSTCARD

*The monastery at Rila,
founded by Ivan Rilski
in 946.*

I saw a man
drown in six
inches of water,

and with the next
wave his body
disappeared.

It was nothing
like Emily Dickinson.
His neck broke like a

pretzel, and before I
could get to him
he was gone.

I was the only witness,
though his girl watched
from shore.

It was a theft
you had to see
to believe.

I was happy
to say goodbye
to Varna.

Take care
of yourself
and the family.

— after Greg Gatenby, October, 1982

# TWO SEAS

## I  PLASENCIA

All arms and legs, storks land like paratroopers
on the huge nests that crown the cathedral towers.

This town is home to Joaquin, Granadan Jew,
who fled Franco twenty-six years ago

for South America. Now he is back
— to run a campground in the Castilian hills

(studded, like cloved hams, with olive trees)
and treat his favoured guests to rich *rioja alta*

and fine philosophy: "Three questions:
who are we, what are we, why are we here?"

and "Madrid? You are going to Madrid?
It is shitty. You will open your eyes."

Packhorses carry cherries at Rio Jerte.
Scalped trunks of cork trees are the burnt orange

of sponge toffee. Eagles hang like gliders
over the vineyards, the almond groves.

## II  MADRID

We move from a mugging on Plaza Mayor
(a man in a red shirt running down an alley,

 bellowing) to Goya's "Autumn, or The Vintage".
Imitation here is an art: a half-finished copy

stands on an easel in front of the real thing;
four hundred miles away, another version — vast,

bad — hangs in the one-star Hotel Trujillo,
in Jerez.  In "Adoration of the Shepherds"

you can see El Greco's influence on Thomas Hart Benton,
the "clamorous mannerist colours"*; you can see

"the Velasquez of the small maids of honor"**
and his portraits of the vain inbred Felipe IV;

you can see Pradilla's "La Reina Dona Juana,
'La Loca'": the watchful maids-in-waiting;

the infanta's sad attempt to engage her mother
with toys; the mad queen herself — her haunted eyes.


\*   Jose Antonio de Urbina, *The Prado: Spanish Paintings*, 1988
\*\* Ernest Hemingway, *Death in the Afternoon*, 1932

## III  TARIFA

Waiting in line at the bank, a crippled girl
selling Loteria from a clip at her collar

does a brisk business.  Here where the muscular
wind blows rooftop laundry horizontal, hunchbacks

are as common as surfers.  Boys boogie-board
where waves break, and bare-breasted women

lean back on their elbows in the sand.
Off Isla de Las Palomas, where the two seas meet,

I snorkel above a headless doll and a painted eel.
An artist, Jose Luis, leads us through narrow streets

of stray cats, jasmine and clicking castanets
to the tapas bars inside the Arab wall:

El Coto, Point Bar, Bar Rico; in the harbour
the tuna boats *Virgen de la Luz* and *Mar Rojo*

bob at their moorings.  Across the dark 'dos mares'
Africa sleeps on her side like a giant.

## IV  TANGIER

Mustapha guides us to a carpet emporium
and disappears while Hassan and company go to work

on us ("My final offer, my friend, and I swear
 on my religion I shall not profit a single dirham"),

then runs for cover in the casbah
when a young man whose T-shirts we refuse

mocks us: "Don't trust anybody?  Don't trust anybody?
This is not Chicago!"  We squeeze past piles

of reeking fish and meat, mountains of paprika
and yellow turmeric, lemons brilliant in a square

of sunlight, a Berber water-seller in red tunic
and goat fur, blind men led by children.

In the old American embassy (Mustapha, too,
 mistakes us for Americans) we study Caton Woodville's

woodcut engravings of the British Mission, while
Mustapha waits outside with a band of beggar musicians.

## V  LISBON

On the road to Portalegre, a gypsy caravan
stops for repairs; three horses and a mule

wait patiently in their places; two boys
with caramel faces sit high atop the wagon

— a breeze blows their blueblack hair.
An hour away, old women peer from behind

the curtain-doors of tiny homes clawed
into the walls of the hilltop castle

at Campo Maior; the cobble streets
are spotless, and everything smells

of burnt sugar — like the flan at Botin's.
In the Jumbo Mall in Setubal

I have a McFrango (in Madrid it's a McPollo).
In our hotel room, we drink our

little fridge's beer.  Our flight is at nine.
The night man will wake us at seven.

## VI  L'ENVOI

Last night I dreamed my father was alive.
I was in his living-room, sorting through

doubles of photos I had taken, choosing
those I thought my mother would like

— the Roman ruins at Bolonia, *vaqueros*
running their cattle under the highway;

the bullring at La Linea, Gibraltar
rising behind it like a leviathan.

He was sitting opposite me, animated,
his silver hair brushed straight back

from his forehead.  "You look good,"
I said. "This is such a surprise.

We miss you." But he didn't respond
and when I awoke  — a motorbike ripping

the night apart, the wind just stirring
beside me — I was still in Spain.